BIRDS

Troll Associates

BIRDS

by Laurence Santrey

Illustrated by Pamela Johnson

Troll Associates

Library of Congress Cataloging in Publication Data

Santrey, Laurence.
  Birds.

  Summary: Briefly traces the development of birds
and describes some of the many species living today.
    1. Birds—Juvenile literature.   [1. Birds]   I. Johnson,
Pamela, ill.   II. Title.
QL676.2.S35   1985   598   84-2731
ISBN 0-8167-0192-X (lib. bdg.)
ISBN 0-8167-0193-8 (pbk.)

Birds are among the most interesting and beautiful creatures in our world. Some are small enough to hold in your hand. Some have feathers as glorious as a rainbow. Some sing wonderfully sweet songs. From the tiny, fragile hummingbird to the majestic eagle to the giant ostrich, the world of birds is a fascinating one.

Archaeopteryx

Even before mammals walked the earth, there were birds. Scientists tell us that the first bird, archaeopteryx, lived 150 million years ago. But it didn't look very much like any of the birds alive today. It looked more like a lizard with feathers. In fact, archaeopteryx is believed to be the link between birds and reptiles.

Archaeopteryx had a long backbone that jutted out behind it, the way a lizard's tail sticks out in back. And it had a thin jaw with sharp teeth. But, like a bird, it had wings, and its tail was feathered.

In the millions of years since archaeopteryx flew, there have been many changes in the structure and appearance of birds. They have developed strong breastbones and shoulder bones. Their tails have grown shorter, and their legs have grown longer.

And over the course of time their bones have become thinner and hollow, their wings bigger and stronger. All these changes made it possible for birds to fly faster, higher, and farther.

Sometime in the distant past other changes took place. Reptiles and their early bird relations had small brains, weak eyes, and sharp teeth. The birds' brains grew larger, and their eyes grew much sharper.

Falcon

Canary

Parakeet

And, as their feeding habits changed, they lost the need for teeth. Modern birds are toothless.

There are many different species of birds today. Some, such as the penguin, the ostrich, and the chicken, are considered to be nonflying birds. Some, like the canary and the parakeet, make good pets. And some, like the eagle and the falcon, are fierce predators.

But all birds—from the little brown sparrow you see in the park to the penguins that waddle over the ice in Antarctica—have certain things in common.

All birds have wings. All birds have beaks or bills. All birds also have feathers. And they all are *oviparous*, which means that their young are hatched from hard-shelled eggs. But different kinds of birds look very different, live in different places, eat different foods, and protect themselves in different ways.

House sparrow

What makes it possible for the common house sparrow to survive so well? This small, brown bird feeds on the ground, so its colors are a perfect camouflage when it hops over the dirt. It has a short, cone-shaped beak that is just right for cracking open seeds and catching insects.

The house sparrow can live in cities and suburbs and forests. It will eat almost anything. It nests in deserted birdhouses, on the ledges of buildings, in trees and shrubs, and in practically any kind of hollow place.

What's more, except for the very hottest and coldest parts of the world, the house sparrow can survive in any climate.

Many species of birds cannot survive in the varied conditions that the sparrow can. When winter cold reduces their food supply, these species must travel to warmer climates until spring comes again. This yearly trip to the south in autumn and back north in the spring is called *migration*. Canada geese, robins, and the ruby-throated hummingbird are migratory birds that fly thousands of miles twice every year.

Migratory birds know just when it is time to start their long flight. This knowledge is an *instinct*, something they do not have to be taught. Migratory birds are born with the instinct to migrate.

In the autumn, as the days grow shorter and the sun rides lower in the sky, the migratory instinct turns on, and many species take to the air for the flight south.

Canada geese

Some species of birds, such as robins and starlings, are mainly day migrants. They fly during the hours of light and settle down to rest at night.

Most species of day-migrating birds make their journeys in large groups. These birds use their sharp vision to guide them on their way. Rivers, forests, and coastlines are landmarks they recognize from the air. These tell the migrating birds they are following the right path.

Other birds, such as warblers and vesper sparrows, are night-migrating birds. Birds that migrate at night use the night sky, with its pattern of stars, as a map to guide them in the right direction. During the day they feed and rest. When the night sky is overcast with clouds that block out the stars, the night-fliers stay on the ground.

The paths migrating birds follow are called *flyways*. Flyways are not narrow, well-marked roads, like our highways. Flyways are wide bands of air space high above the ground and are used by many species of migrating birds.

Every spring the flyways are filled with birds heading back north for the summer. They are returning now because instinct tells them to do so. Once the birds have returned to their northern homes, it is time for them to choose a mate. The spring air is filled with lovely bird songs and calls. The males sing to the females, and the females answer back in song.

In some species of birds the male struts, puffs out his feathers, or does a kind of dance to catch a female's attention. Some birds choose mates for the season, while the birds of other species remain with the same mates all their lives.

Each pair of birds finds a good place to build a nest. It must be safe from wind and weather and from natural enemies. Each species has its own kind of nest. The lark builds a nest among stones on the ground.

Blue jay

Hairy woodpecker

Grebe

King penguin

The water bird called the grebe builds a floating nest in a pond. The hairy woodpecker builds its nest in the hollow of a tree. And the blue jay builds its nest on a high branch of a tree.

To build a nest, birds use straw, twigs, rags, grass, mud, paper, moss, and just about anything else that fits the need. The African tailorbird sews together leaves with grass and spider silk and stuffs this nest with soft grass. The Adélie penguin piles up stones on the ice of its nesting grounds to form a protected area for its eggs.

As soon as the nests are ready, egg-laying begins. Most small birds lay about four eggs at a time. Some species lay only one egg, while others lay as many as twenty. Bird eggs come in many sizes, from the hummingbird egg that is the size of your fingernail to the ostrich egg that's almost as big as a football. The eggs may be white, green, blue, black, brown, or dotted with colors.

In some species of birds, the parents take turns sitting on the eggs until they hatch. In other species only one parent sits on the egg.

This sitting is also called *incubation* or *brooding*. The parent broods the eggs to keep them warm and turns the eggs regularly so they will develop evenly. The other parent may sit on the ground or on a nearby branch, guarding the nest. Or it may go hunting for food to bring back to its mate.

Once the baby birds hatch, they must be cared for until they are ready to look after themselves. The parents feed them and protect them from enemies. The parents also show the nestlings how to search for food.

Once the young birds are big and strong enough to get around by themselves, they are on their own. This growing-up time is different for different kinds of birds. But most young birds are on their own before autumn.

The main activity of grown-up birds is finding food. That is because birds use up their food quickly and must keep eating to stay alive. Some species of birds eat only seeds and berries. Other species eat worms, caterpillars, and small insects, as well as seeds and berries.

The water birds eat fish, frogs, shellfish, and plants, often diving or ducking their heads underwater to feed. Many large birds, such as the owl and eagle, are predators. That means they swoop down and catch small mammals, snakes, and other birds.

Feeding itself is the center of a bird's life. For this reason, where the bird nests and how it spends its time depends on its feeding habits and needs. Even its body structure must be adapted to these demands. For example, many large water birds have long, sharp beaks perfect for catching fish. And the hummingbird's needle-thin beak and tube-like tongue are ideal for sipping nectar from flowers.

Green heron

A bird's body is very well designed for all its needs. The wings of flying birds are beautifully streamlined. The wing feathers are connected by rows of little hooks, forming a strong, flexible instrument for flight. Birds do not fly by simply flapping their wings up and down. Instead, the wings are brought up, forward, down, and back.

Shaft

Hook

The colors of a bird's feathers are also important. Birds can recognize others of their species by color. A bird like the peacock uses a show of beautiful feathers to attract a mate.

And by using color as camouflage, some birds are able to hide from their enemies by blending in with their surroundings. One bird, the ptarmigan, even turns white during the winter and blends in with the snow.

There are more than 8,000 different kinds of birds on earth. Each one has some way to defend itself. Each has its own kind of nest and its own special coloring. Each also has its own special voice. When you hear a *quack*, you know that a duck is nearby. When you hear a *honk-honk*, you can be sure that some geese are not too far away.

Wren

Other birds may not be quite as easy to identify by their voices, but it's fun to try. And even if you don't know what kind of bird is singing, you can always enjoy listening to their songs!

30